I0468566

GAY:

What does the Bible really say?

A Reverend's Philosophy in Support of the Gay Community

By Reverend Anna Grace

CreateSpace Independent Publishing Platform, North
Charleston, SC
2016 LCCN#2016906139

May the Truth Set You Free

Table of Contents

Chapter 1 – The Origins of Our Perceptions About Homosexuality

Gay. What does the Bible *really* say? One might think this a strange title for a book because quite frankly we all *know* what the bible really says about homosexuality, right? Well, actually we all *think* we have a clear idea about what the bible really says about homosexuality, right? Perhaps it is also strange to have a Reverend writing a book in support of the gay community. In fact, only three years ago, my writings would have been strongly opposed to the homosexual and/or LGBT community all together.

Fortunately, something happened over the past few years through hours of study and reflection and investigation and research. I have had an epiphany of truth, and my desire now is to retract all the negative energy and discriminatory sentiments that I was emitting from my heart and mind for so many years. I have discovered absolute irrefutable proof that what I believed previously about homosexuality was in complete contrast to the actual truth of God. My hope now is to help those who are oppressed or rejected by their communities or churches or families or friends for their sexual orientation by teaching them the undeniable facts as written in scripture. I want to help to provide a substantial foundation for those who often find themselves pressed into debate with others regarding the morality of homosexuality. I present the evidence here of what is already known in the heart: God loves all and accepts all persons just the way they are, and so should everyone else.

My daughter, who is gay, says that the most commonly voiced dismissal she receives against her sexual orientation from peers and others is, "It's against my religion." We, my daughter and I, live in an overwhelmingly Christian community, and I am here to tell this community honestly, "No, it is definitely not against the Christian religion to be gay."

Gays are looked down upon in many sects of society because society's foundational beliefs about homosexuality, which most likely stem from an overshadowing residual belief in Biblical principles, are that homosexuality is wrong. My hypothesis in this book is not that the Bible is against homosexuality, but that society's actual *interpretation* about the Biblical principles are wrong, and the Bible does not actually say what society thinks it says about homosexuality. Let us therefore begin to change our beliefs about sexual orientation by learning the truth of what the religious opinion *should* be about the subject according to Biblical *truth*, at least the religious opinion of those who honor the Bible.

We have most likely heard this following statement repeatedly at several junctures in our lives, to the point where it now echos loudly within our souls: **For a man to lie with another man is an abomination to God**. This is an emotionally-charged judgment-filled statement, which is not to be taken lightly.

Not simply is this act of a man lying with another man distasteful or displeasing to God. Make no bones about it. This act is an *abomination* to God. And things get even worse when we look at the actual text as found in Leviticus chapter 20 and verse 13. "If a man also lie with mankind, as he lieth with a woman, both of them have committed an abomination: they shall surely be put to death; their blood *shall be* upon them." Death. *Death* is the punishment for such an *abominable* act of homosexuality.

So we see God's firm position against the homosexual community, and we model our very societal standards and ethics regarding this subject around God's unyielding and obvious aversion to homosexuality. In this practice of modeling civil morality on the Bible is where the basis for this book lies. We, as a society, have shapen our ethical ideologies regarding sexuality according to God's law as found written in the Bible.

As we take a close look at scripture, we are going to discover that in many parts of the world opinions and biases, beliefs and judgments regarding what is morally right and what is morally wrong have developed from some foundational beliefs taken from the Bible. Though one might not even affiliate with a certain religion, many societal structures are not only influenced by but substantiated upon civil and legislative principles found in the Bible. It is of critical importance then that we examine the criteria, philosophy, and standards of the Bible, as it has had such a tremendous persuasion upon modern civilization.

What we have established through the homosexual standards in the Bible is a sentiment of repugnance and disdain towards homosexuality. If God himself can not tolerate homosexuality, neither should we, and hence, many in society don't. Though the Western World no longer puts gays to death, the assumed attitude of much of society has been strong nonacceptance, if not total prejudice and rejection and hatred.

Not only has common civilization been effected by these powerful dispositions, but many religious systems are deeply entrenched in negative opinions against the gay community. Even though the Christian church does not put to death those who are gay, they usually still have a staunch and uncompromising stance against homosexuality. We also note this same principle in the Islamic faith, where homosexuality is forbidden and unacceptable. As three major religions in the world which stem from Biblical principles promote the same intolerant position, the gay community has been persecuted and misrepresented for many millennia in many parts of the world.

All that being said, one may find many adherents to these aforementioned faiths who do not wholeheartedly agree with the rejection of gay people. Though one might consider himself 'religious,' he or she may know and love a gay person without judgment, or may even be gay themselves. Over the years, some small sects have undoubtedly changed their opinion on the subject of homosexuality. In certain areas and populations now, it may even be considered quite taboo to reject a person for his or her sexual orientation. At the same time, there are many fundamentalists and/or conservatives who yet completely renounce this sexual lifestyle.

Sexual orientation is definitely a controversial subject, with tremendously robust opinions on both sides of the coin. The sole intention of this book is to get to the root of the religious and civil opinion regarding homosexuality and to determine how the Bible *actually* manages this subject. Has society as a whole really come to the foundational conclusion about what the scripture truly says? Though we have already quoted one verse from the Bible regarding homosexual law, there are approximately 29,999 other verses to contemplate regarding God's opinions.

The hypothesis posited here is that if we can come to a decisive answer about God's perspective on this subject, which will ultimately equate with finding the very source of our own sentiments, we may be able to conclude the debate over the customs and traditions of negative homosexual treatment in our society. As has occurred in the past, if God's beliefs are known, society often follows in line with God's beliefs.

Here in the United States, the very framework of our legal and social structures are built upon the precedence of God's word and God's commandments and God's laws as outlined in the Bible. In fact, much of the Western World stands on the basis of the Biblical archetype for societal principles and structures as demonstrated all the way back to Moses. Not only do we take our beliefs about homosexuality from the ordinances given in the Old Testament, many governmental and legal systems today operate via the model of God's law.

Why do we adhere to the patterns and prototypes in the Bible? Well, those very principles are supposed to lead us to heaven, are they not? If we follow these patterns and laws as outlined in the Bible, the promise is that they will lead us to the Promised Land where everyone can live in peace, harmony, love, and acceptance of all. And so, the theory is, if we follow the outline of these rules, we will have a harmonious and heavenly society.

Chapter 2 – God's Legal Systems: Pervasive in the Modern World

In the Old Testament, God through Moses set up a system of governance over the Israelites. God gave his ordinances, statutes, and commandments which included approximately 613 laws, rules, and regulations. We, as a society, are very familiar with at least ten of those commandments. If a person were to break one of those laws, such as the sexual law outlined in Chapter 1 of this book, the usual punishment was death, exile or retribution equal to the loss incurred by the crime. We see a similar legislative structure in our court rooms today. If a person breaks a rule, he can expect a sentence similar to one of these disciplinary actions – a fine or retribution, exile from society by incarceration, or death. This same Old Testament system of criminal activity, trial before the law, and retribution for the crime is followed in most first world countries today.

Likewise, God's word not only defines a legislative and judicial philosophy, but also delineates a set of religious laws, statutes, and commandments. God ordered a series of priestly practices which included rituals of service to God, sacrifices for God, and obedience to a moral set of rules. These practices allowed for the priests and the congregation to become righteous or holy enough to dwell in the presence of God. So we also deduce today that if we follow God's legal system and his religious system, we are able to dwell in godliness.

Moses, through God's commands, set up a religious rite which is still practiced in the modern Christian church today. High priests still serve and minister to God for the masses, performing certain rituals to keep themselves clean and holy, such as partaking of holy bread. This ritual was first ordained in Moses' law, with a holy bread called *shewbread*. The church community, as in Moses' law, was to tithe a portion of their wealth to the church so that the priests could have sustenance. This is still practiced in churches today. There are truly too many parallels to list between today's multitude of Christian denominational traditions and Biblical practices. These religions feign separateness, but are ultimately tied to the same root through similar foundational beliefs and similar practices as outlined in the Bible. How distinct could they actually be, if their one and only instruction comes from the same book?

Thus, God's legal and judicial systems and religious frameworks are the foundations of our societal practices today. We believe the Bible is a guide or book of instructions, and through our belief, we accept a set of social, civil, legal, and religious customs and traditions. If we dig a little further into the 613 commands given by God, we would even see a set of principles related to international commerce and foreign policy.

In his book, A Handbook of Bible Law, Charles Weisman states, "While fair and peaceable interrelations between nations were the norm, God had prohibited any interaction, trade, aid or treaties to be conducted with ungodly nations." One can obviously see a little bit of ambiguity in this law, for what defines an ungodly nation back then may not define an ungodly nation now. Religious belief or attestation of God might have little to nothing to do with international relations today from a Western standpoint, as we have aided all types of nations. However, we still believe in fair and peaceable relations with other countries. Weisman goes on to say, "The biblical guidelines concerning foreign relations were well expressed by Presidents Washington and Jefferson who said we should have peace, commerce, and honesty with nations, are to avoid entangling alliances with all nations and should not allow any foreign influence in our land." We understand that our founding fathers definitely relied upon Biblical guidance for all aspects of government.

However, there are certainly other nations in the world who similarly use Biblical principles as a guideline or starting point for their own governmental, legislative, international, or religious systems, picking and choosing (whether wittingly or unwittingly) from the main precepts and ideas of the book. Quite honestly, the Bible covers all of these disciplines so thoroughly, anyone who would endeavor to found a sovereign nation would be hard pressed to deviate substantially from Biblical principle.

Everything from the rules for strategies of war to the treatment of widows can be found within the pages of the Bible. It is one of the earliest and most comprehensive documents regarding civil structure and law, and the best selling text ever. To say it is simply a Holy Book dealing with religion would be outrageously understated. Its far and wide reaching influence should not be disregarded. Talk about the long, long arm of the law...

Though the diverse countries of the world sometimes appear radically different from outside examination, if one were to take a fine tooth comb to analyze the base of their governments, what would be revealed is that most of their principles could be substantiated in one section of the bible or another, from the most fascist to the more liberal.

The foundation of our very civilization stands upon the practices, standards, and statutes organized through God's law of commandments, but it would be impossible for any nation to abide by each and every law delineated in scripture. Though many nations may be founded on the Bible's principles as far as structure, those same nations certainly don't implement each individual miniscule law. Many laws from the Old Testament are today abolished and eradicated all together.

For instance, it would be quite surprising if a church, any church, were to take it upon themselves to slaughter the obscene number of animals required by the system of God's sacrificial law. This practice seems not only primitive and barbaric, but completely impractical and useless. Yet, on the other hand, many people do still abide by the sentiment of the law which states that homosexuality is an atrocious sin. This dichotomy is true for the rest of the 600 plus laws, and so our system seems to be built upon a bit of hypocrisy. Either we follow the structure of laws and precepts in the Bible, or we do not follow the structure of laws and precepts in the Bible.

It was said that following those regulations would result in a society that could exist with harmony, love, and security. Perhaps we should be more stringent in our adherence to all the laws of the Bible, or perhaps we need to wholly abolish them all together. If we don't go as far as to follow every detailed law, especially those regarding daily rituals because they are impractical and useless, perhaps the foundation those laws are based upon is also impractical and useless.

One thing is certain regarding this dichotomy; living within the midst of obedience to some of the laws and ignorance of the other half of the laws both has not delivered us to a smoothly functioning heavenly community. Should we take on the homosexual law and the other laws with even more gusto and determination to see if we indeed can create a heavenly community in doing so? Or should we abolish our demeaning opinions about gays by getting rid of all the laws of the Old Testament as we have disregarded other laws of the Old Testament?

Fortunately, in history we have an example of a society who strictly adhered to each and every law "religiously." The Jewish community had made a legally binding covenant with God through Moses that they would keep each and every law as ordained in the Old Testament. At Mount Sinai when presented with these laws, the Jewish people contracted with God in Exodus 19:8, "And all the people answered together, and said, All that the LORD hath spoken we will do. And Moses returned the words of the people unto the LORD." God in turn promised to give the people a land flowing with milk and honey. You guessed it – the proverbial Promised Land of paradise, peace, and rest is the reward for the people who follow the LORD's laws.

Yet, we have not even begun to touch upon the teachings of the New Testament. So now, through the writings of the New Testament, let's look in hind sight at what actually happened to the Jewish nation. Hind sight is 20/20, and the New Testament Jews have a lot to discuss when it comes to how the Israelites fared when abiding by all the laws and commandments in their Torah. Let's begin with the most famous Jew of the New Testament, Jesus Christ.

Chapter 3 – Enter Jesus Christ

Though Moses brought us the structure for our secular and religious legislative systems, we have not yet introduced these same disciplines as taught in the New Testament. In keeping with the theme of the last chapter, we must admit that even every good Bible-believing Christian doesn't follow each trivial law of old. Perhaps this is because we understand that Jesus came to be the sacrificial lamb for the world, and so at least we can validate the abolition of the law of animal sacrifice, and many of the other laws through Jesus' death. It is stated that Jesus has satisfied the ritual requirement for blood sacrifice. Let us further investigate what Jesus says about following the legally binding laws and ordinances of the Old Testament.

Jesus said in Matt 5:17, "Think not that I am come to destroy the law, or the prophets: I am not come to destroy, but to fulfil." To fulfill means to satisfy all requirements and obligations. Accomplish, achieve, complete, realize, meet, answer, fill, end, terminate, conclude. Which laws and requirements did Jesus come to fulfill? Which ordinances and commandments did Jesus come to terminate? Which principles and beliefs did Jesus come to answer? Out of the 613 commands, which are we still to abide by and which have been satisfied?

To pick through the Old Testament to determine which obligations are still necessary and which are put to rest by Jesus seems a monumental task. Let's put this in perspective. The Old Testament says regarding a criminal act, an eye for an eye and a tooth for a tooth. Does our legal system abide by this law? Yes, when a criminal is named and charged and convicted, he must repay through fines or jail time according to what is deemed to be equivalent to the pain incurred by his crime. Of course, sometimes murder requires the death of the perpetrator. Does our religious structure still require that we serve God as Moses and all of his ministers did in the Old Testament? Yes, all of us must serve God and do good deeds if we want to be "accounted worthy" (Luke 20:35) to get into heaven. So what has Jesus come to fulfill?

What of this law in the Old Testament? Exodus 31:15 states, "Six days may work be done; but in the seventh is the sabbath of rest, holy to the LORD:

whosoever doeth any work in the sabbath day, he shall surely be put to death." Do we kill people, or is it even deemed 'illegal' to work on a Saturday? Of course not. Jesus must have fulfilled this requirement. And this, as stated in Leviticus 11:12, "Whatsoever hath no fins nor scales in the waters, that shall be an abomination unto you." This ordinance declares shrimp and lobster need be off our menus. Jesus must have fulfilled this law because we don't obey this one. Exodus 21:17 commands, "And he that curseth his father, or his mother, shall surely be put to death." Luckily, Jesus fulfilled this one or every teenager would be on death row.

Our real life examples above that Jesus has fulfilled some of the laws, but not all of them. For instance, the Ten Commandments are religiously taught in Christian churches around the globe. Interesting dichotomy again, as this seems to be an oxymoron and a bit hypocritcal. So, perhaps the better angle should be to investigate *why* Jesus came to fulfill the laws from the Old Testament?

The fundamental principle here which completely escapes Christianity in the Western World is the fact that all of these rules from Jehovah through

Moses were holding the Jews to a very restrictive, very tedious, and very laborious set of legally binding requirements. Jesus came to fulfill these old rules, precisely because they were holding the Jewish nation in bondage. Haven't we heard that Jesus came to set the prisoners free?

What was holding the people in captivity? The same thing that holds people in prison today – the law, the legal system, both civil and religious. Under the Biblical principle, one is *bound* to uphold his end of the contract (which is to follow the laws), in order that God uphold his end of the contract (which is to give us peace in the heavenly land).

The Jewish priests and the Jewish community both were striving and toiling in service or servitude to God, desperately trying to accomplish the entirety of the letter of the law down to every miniscule "jot and tittle." All of these requirements consumed their lives, holding them bound by their legal contract with God. They had agreed in a mutually binding covenant to adhere to every law so that they could inherent a land flowing with milk and honey, and this very law had put them in bondage to accomplish the whole of 613 impossible tasks. New Testament scripture says in

Gal 4:24 "...the one [covenant] from the mount Sinai, which gendereth to *bondage*."

So Jesus came to set the Jews free from this bondage. Yet, now we, through our religious and/or legislative system have taken on a similar burden, for we still abide by the foundational principles of some of these rules. We still believe that if we behave appropriately and serve faithfully and punish the criminals accordingly, we can earn our place in the Promised Land of Heaven. We still believe that if we implement laws and punish criminals our society can be harmonious and peaceful. We simply don't understand that the Savior actually had come to save us from these very principles and doctrines which dictate that following these precepts and maintaining good behavior according to those precepts, is the way to a heavenly community.

Not only was the Law holding the people in captivity through the immensely taxing daily rituals, the principles behind the law were causing the people to be discriminatory. If a person was found to be in noncompliance with all 613 tediously intricate requirements, he was shunned from society or demeaned in the community. The law is what gave the society a basis for judging some as good and others as bad. This ideology reveals that some were indeed somehow degenerate or evil while others were holy, righteous, and special. The law, and only the law, cast a negative light on some behaviors, or lack of behaviors, making it possible for discrimination to arise. This is where not only do the tedious daily miniscule laws begin to crumble, but the foundation of this system begins to crumble, which we will talk about in the next chapter.

Romans 7:9-11 sums up the corruption caused by the Old System, "For I was alive without the law once: but when the commandment came, sin revived, and I died. And the commandment, which was ordained to life, I found to be unto death. For sin, taking occasion by the commandment, deceived me, and by it slew me." Now, the writer is not actually slain or dead, but is spiritually dead, psychologically crushed by burden of believing in the destructive and discriminatory principles put forth through the law. The entire Jewish society was cursed to not only slave and toil to serve God in servitude, but also cursed by the belief that others were somehow inherently wicked. You see, as stated in Romans 7, they were deceived, and Galatians 3:10 states, "For as many as are of the works of the law are under the curse:"

So in the New Testament, through Jesus and his disciples, we discover that the old laws cause bondage and spiritual death and discrimination, NOT the promised eternal life in a heavenly peaceful community they were supposed to create. The Jewish nation was actually under a curse, and therefore, anyone who still abides by the foundation principles delineated through the law, are under a curse also.

The Bible says in the New Testament that the only way to make it to heaven is through faith in Christ, yet we still try to abide by the laws of Jehovah in order to set up our own heavenly community. We have just proven that adhering to those principles don't lead to heaven, but hell. In following Biblical doctrine, we have actually tainted our society with bondage, death and discrimination. Is there any need to wonder then why there is so much pain and suffering in the world, if much of the whole system is structured around Biblical principles?

The truth is Jesus came to fulfill *all* of these written carnal laws. In effect, none of the laws of the Old Testament need be regarded any longer. Jesus *fulfilled* the law, even the Ten Commandments, for the one written above from Exodus 31:15 about the Sabbath day is part of Commandment number four. The truth is Jesus fulfilled all of the laws, but our society and our churches don't follow that fact and still base their foundational structures and beliefs on the Old Testament framework. One might say that though we believe the Bible, we actually have no faith in Christ, and the homosexual law is a perfect example of this. This is where our hypocrisy is revealed. Christ came to do away with these structures, we just don't practice that in our reality.

We have to ask ourselves if we believe that Jesus fulfilled the laws and requirements and commandments and ordinances of the Old Testament? If the answer is yes, as Jesus did state himself that he came to fulfill it and declared that it was finished with his dying breath at the cross, then there is *no old testament law.* It is fulfilled, satisfied, completed.

This is what the Bible says about the fact that the law is concluded. The Bible actually teaches in Romans 4:15, "For where no law is, there is no transgression." If there is no longer any law to abide by, there is no longer any transgression. If there is no transgression, there are no more criminals. No one is guilty because the law is finished. If there is no law, no one can break it. No one is a sinner, and no one is guilty including homosexuals. That law against homosexuality no longer exists if one believes in Jesus' accomplishment. Jesus fulfilled all the laws, not just some, whether we practice this in our reality or not.

The Bible then, through Jesus, actually teaches there is no ordinance against homosexuality. Scripture says Jesus blotted out the handwriting of all those ordinances, meaning he *erased them* or *whited them out*. We are now free as a society to put to rest that belief that homosexuality is an abomination, and start accepting the homosexual community as Jesus would have. Though our Western philosophy claims that it has been founded upon the truth of the Bible, we simply don't understand that the Bible actually says there is no law against homosexuality, do we? It's time for all that to change.

Chapter 4 – The Truth Will Set You Free

So it is written that Christ came to fulfill the law. It is finished because all the legal system was able to accomplish, according to the Jews themselves from the New Testament, was death, discrimination, and bondage. We will take this one step deeper.

Firstly, we know that Jesus fulfilled the law, rendering the law invalid and so making every person innocent, as there is no longer a set of rules to criminalize anyone with. Jesus has washed away all sins by defeating the law. Where there is no law, there can be no criminals or sinners. No one has to follow those laws any longer.

Here is the second result of Jesus' sacrifice in black and white in Colossians 2:14-15, "having forgiven you all trespasses; Blotting out the handwriting of ordinances that was against us, which was contrary to us, and took it out of the way, nailing it to his cross; And having spoiled principalities and powers, he made a shew of them openly, triumphing over them in it." The translation from Olde English to modern language reveals that when he blotted out the law then, the result was to triumph over the principles and beliefs that were created by the foundational structure of the entire system of law. Read that again slowly, as it is of pivotal importance. The foundational structure of this system of law and punishment creates discrimination, bondage, and spiritual death. And this is where the cookie crumbles.

Discrimination arises when one believes that another is inherently evil or wicked, a bad seed. If one has deviated from the narrow road of obedience, there is then something wrong with that person. He or she is not holy or good enough. So the law calls for his or her exile, or worse, their demise. The foundation of the law has a flaw, as it assumes that if a person is disobedient, he is simply degenerate, lesser of a human being, evil. Through Jesus' teachings, however, we will see that this is not even close to the truth.

In addition, through law, minds began to believe incorrectly in wickedness. Ask yourself one simple question: Do the religious see righteousness in everyone? No! Absolutely not. They see the sin in everyone else because their religious laws have taught them what unholiness is. Are homosexuals good in the eyes of the religious? No, they are bad because they go against the law. The Bible even says that the religious sit in thrones judging the nations. They can judge and condemn because they know Law! What they actually need to know is Christ.

Remember Romans 7:11, "For sin, taking occasion by the commandment *deceived* me, and by it slew me." Listen to what scripture has to say about that deceived mind set in Titus 1:15, "Unto the pure, all things are pure, but unto them that are defiled is nothing pure." If those with the religious mindset were actually pure themselves, they would see purity in all things, even homosexuality. They would not see evil in everyone and everywhere in the world. If you have ever listened to even one fiery sermon from a pulpit you have heard of all the sins and wickedness out in the world. Ironically, it is the knowledge they have of the law that has revealed what is wrong with everyone else. Having the knowledge, then of what is evil, makes them evil. The law has deceived them into seeing evil everywhere. That deception has caused impurity and evil within the law-abiding person himself. It takes a sinner to know sin. It takes wickedness to know evil. I know this is all a confounding riddle, this is why Jesus spoke in parables. And this is also why most people have not figured these principles out yet.

And so the deceptive principles of the Bible have tainted the entire world's view with falsehood and lie. These laws simply do not lead to God, the Promised Land, purity, peace or truth. Instead they were a curse upon the peoples. All they proved to do is cause bondage, death, strife, discrimination, fear, and judgment. The Bible itself states that no man can be justified, nor good enough, nor declared innocent by doing the works of the law, for the law always reveals sin thereby making him guilty always, Romans 3:19-20. Gal 2:21 says, "for if righteousness come by the law, then Christ is dead in vain."

Though modern religious doctrine will tell you that Jesus came to save the world from sin, the deeper truth is that the way the sin was only "washed away" because Jesus erased *the laws* that revealed what was sinful. So Jesus actually came to save the world from the law: the sin only being a byproduct of the law. Wash away the sins by getting rid of the law. Now that there is no law, one does not have to believe that a person committing an act of homosexuality is sinful. That misguided principle is triumphed over.

Likewise, now that there is no law against

coveting your neighbors goods (Commandment #10), you don't have to believe that someone is evil because they desire to have a similar red convertible Cadillac parked in their driveway as their neighbor has. The principle that states that a person is immoral for coveting is all wrong. Coveting does not make a person inherently abominable, sinful, evil, or inferior. Jesus revealed the truth: Get rid of those laws, there are no transgressors, and therefore no reason to discriminate.

Knowing the truth sets us free from the bondage of having to discriminate against or dislike or demean homosexuals. Jesus showed repeatedly that God wouldn't do that, nor should anyone else. It is now okay to accept, respect, and love all persons equally.

One doesn't have to be clean, pure, and holy to dwell with God as the Bible would have one believe. The foundational principle of that belief is wrong. Jesus, in portraying the Truth and the Way, demonstrated that God indeed dwells among the lowly, the unrighteous and the sickly. We all know that Jesus kept company with the criminals, thieving tax collectors, and prostitutes, and chose them over the holy and 'clean' religious group. It is simply not true that God (as revealed by the Son of God) doesn't approve of the so-called sinful. Again, as demonstrated through Jesus, God simply does not discriminate, even though the structure of this legal system deceives us into believing he would discriminate by sending some to hell, and giving heaven to the holy.

Jesus taught that the Promised Land is within, and the only way to get there is by loving everyone, not by behaving well. Jesus gave us two new commandments. In summation, they read like this: Love God, and Love your neighbor as yourself. Wouldn't these new laws lead us to the Promised Community?

So, are you still convinced the homosexual statute is valid and that following it and believing in it is of some benefit to anyone, including yourself?

It is true that if you still believe in this law against homosexuality and believe it is a sin (or morally wrong), you have no faith in Christ because Christ came to blot out this law (and all the others) and take away the sins of the world by doing such. If you abide still by the homosexual law and judge homosexuals as inferior in some manner, the truth is that *you* would be the sinner for having no faith in what Christ taught. James 2:9says, "But if ye have respect to persons, ye commit sin, and are *convinced of the law as transgressors*."

Are you judging gays as bad or evil because society through the principles of Biblical law says it is so? Then you yourself, being convinced that law is valid, are a transgressor (one who is bad or evil). If you still uphold the law, you don't have faith that Christ fulfilled it, and so because faith is the only righteousness required to 'get to heaven,' you are in fact guilty in God's eyes. The Bible says we are actually justified (accounted worthy in God's eyes) by faith in Christ only. What a riddle this all turns out to be.

Chapter 5 – New Beliefs, New System

If what is purported in the previous chapter is true, according to Jesus we are left without a civil and religious structure, for the old foundational laws are done away with. Contrastingly, and perhaps unfortunately, our systems today still uphold many of the foundational beliefs of the Old Testament. Jesus, as we have discovered, actually came to blot out that governing system of law. That's right. If you know anything about Jesus Christ, he was at odds (to put it mildly) with the religious system, and was put to death by the civil system. Neither system were agreeable to the teachings of Christ.

Yes, it seems that Jesus was a radical thinker who went against the governing systems of the day, which were both based on the foundational systems of the Bible. He fought with the leaders of the Jewish religion, and he again was put to death by the legal system of the Romans. Granted, the Romans did not have the Jewish laws and texts, but their legislative system was based on the exact same premises as described in the Old Testament law.

So, we are left with questioning what kind of system Jesus proposes for our civilization. What was it that Jesus was suggesting if he was adamantly against the political and religious structures of the day (which modeled Old Testament principles)? If carnal laws and rules and regulations from the Old Testament doctrines put us into bondage and spiritual death, how is one supposed to be governed and kept in check in modern society? If carnal laws only reveal the sinful nature of criminals, making them always outcast degenerates, how can we change these systems? If we want to be set free from our servitude, let us examine what Jesus came to reveal about law.

Though what will be presented here seems idealistic, the greatest minds who ever lived have agreed with what Jesus teaches. Please understand that few have understood this hidden wisdom within Jesus' system, and understand that no nation in the world has followed Jesus' ideas up until this point. It is yet to be seen if Jesus' philosophy would bring about the Promised Utopia. The only thing we can surmise is that, as demonstrated throughout history and up until modern times, the Old Testament system has not brought forth a harmonious society.

To begin to comprehend the new ruling system, which is called the *spiritual law* and the *new covenant* in the New Testament, a summary of the incident in John 8 will be analyzed:

"They say unto him [Jesus], Master, this woman was taken in adultery, in the very act. Now Moses in the law commanded us, that such should be stoned: but what sayest thou? So when they continued asking him, he lifted up himself, and said unto them, He that is without sin among you, let him first cast a stone at her. And they which heard it, being convicted by *their own conscience*, went out one by one, beginning at the eldest, even unto the last: and Jesus was left alone, and the woman standing in the midst. When Jesus had lifted up himself, and saw none but the woman, he said unto her, Woman, where are those thine accusers? hath no man condemned thee? She said, No man, Lord. And Jesus said unto her, Neither do I condemn thee:"

Though the old carnal law of Moses demanded that the people stone this woman to death (and our social system today still condemns this act at least by ridicule and mockery and shame), Jesus proposed something new. Jesus knew that all of those participating in this public berating had also committed sin. In asking the first perfect man to pick up the first stone, he knew that this woman could be set free. She would not be condemned to death. She would be forgiven and given back her life.

When Jesus so callously yet carefully presented them with the fact that all could theoretically be stoned because not one had been without sin, their conscience convicted them. Here is the turning point in our understanding. This group of peers felt guilty, convicted by their *conscience* that they were about to commit a heinous act of murder according to their law. They realized suddenly that the law had told them to do something evil. Their conscience, on the other hand, was telling them the truth – 'it is wrong to harm another human being, and I am not perfect either,' said their conscience hypothetically.

The law therefore had lied to them in trying to convey a morally decent way to deal with this situation. To stone is not morally decent, said their conscience. The operative word here is deceived. Their law had deceived them into thinking it was okay to harm another because the person had committed a sin. Fortunately, their conscience was the victor in the fight of morality. Their conscience knew it was wrong to harm another, even though their laws and commandments said to stone in order to correct the wrong that had been committed; and so they left. The conscience instead said do no harm, in essence – forgive.

When we know what to look for, we begin to see this truth all over the scripture. **It is our heart and our conscience which tells us the truth of right and wrong, morality and immorality, ethical practices versus unethical practices, not the principles found in the law of commandments.** Romans 2:14-15 says, "For when the Gentiles, which have not the law, do *by nature* the things contained in the law, these, having not the law, are a law unto themselves: Which shew the work of the law written in their *hearts*, their *conscience* also bearing witness." Again, the summation of these verses tells us that the truth of justice is already written in the hearts and conscience of mankind by our Maker. This law which is written in our hearts *by nature* is called the spiritual law. Law is written in our moral compass of right and wrong, not on a piece of paper in a court of law.

If you truly had to pick up a stone and kill your child for cursing you out, could you do it? Of course not, because your conscience knows this is unjust, and your heart speaks of the love for your child along with your capacity for kindness, forgiveness, and compassion. In this way, our hearts and conscience were meant to be the authority on ethical correctness.

Though most of Christianity believes that Jesus followed the law of Moses, they don't understand that Jesus went beyond the law of Moses into the spiritual law. The example above from John is a perfect criminal case where Jesus went beyond the letter of the law, and actually *broke* the old precept regarding punishment for adultery. The true judge within him ruled to forgive her.

Jesus also said in Luke 6:29, "And unto him that smiteth thee on the one cheek offer also the other; and him that taketh away thy cloke forbid not to take thy coat also." Do you see the difference in Jesus? Instead of punishment for the crime against the law which states "thou shalt not steal", Jesus said let him steal and give him your coat also. A new legal system is presented where the heart judges. If he needs a cloke desperately enough that he would steal for it, help him out and give him your coat also. The Hebrew word for love means to give. Jesus taught love.

Jesus was also accused of breaking the Sabbath day law, Commandment #4. When Jesus answered those accusing him of working on the Sabbath, Jesus recounted that their very own King David broke a law by eating the holy shewbread which was set aside for the priests only. Jesus said that even their own priests had broken the Sabbath day law also. Jesus was simply saying, "Does God really care if you eat bread when you are hungry, when there are literally dozens of loaves to feed the priests who were very well nourished already? Wouldn't it be better to give in charity to one who was starving?" Jesus is prompting the people to think critically, and to show that the truth of the matter is in the heart.

If King David were stealing bread from a poor beggar and her child who had not eaten in two weeks, this might be deemed morally incorrect, and our heart tells us such. However, our conscience also says the law simply doesn't make sense regarding not allowing anyone else to eat the shewbread, for there was plenty share with one who was in need. Why, then, should this be illegal?

Therefore, the law does not have precedence when it comes to judging a person's character. Is David bad because he ate the shewbread? He broke a law, but the law was flawed, not David's intentions. Jesus broke the Sabbath by healing a man's hand. Healing was considered work, and no work was to be done on the Sabbath. Jesus answered, "And he said unto them, What man shall there be among you, that shall have one sheep, and if it fall into a pit on the sabbath day, will he not lay hold on it, and lift *it* out?" Here again, the ethical thing to do is help the animal, and therefore in this case, the law to do no work on the Sabbath is not the highest ethical decision. The conscience and the heart take precedence over the written laws.

Of course, this concept seems ridiculously idealistic to most. However, if you analyze and contemplate the scriptures quoted above, you will see that this, indeed, is truth. In order to believe in the principle of forgiving, listening to your heart, and trusting others no matter their choices in life, you have to believe that there is a light of goodness that lighteth every human who cometh into the world without bias, John 1:9. This means that all men and women are *inherently good* in their hearts, for God has literally written truth and goodness and love in the very fiber of the makeup of the human being. God's signature within every man is literally the life energy that animates humanity. That signature is always loving, always filled with light, for that is the very essence of what God is (1 John 1:5, 1 John 4:8). Every human therefore is good at his core, no matter his or her sexual preference.

What makes mankind appear to be 'evil' is the fact that mankind follows corrupted existential laws which twist a man to act *against* his very nature in some cases. That very signature which God Almighty programmed into man's conscience has to then be denied. For instance, if a man is gay, but he is told this very natural intuition within him is wrong, he becomes confused, feels anxiety, fear, depression, and inferior. This pain and suffering is imposed upon him by a false judgment of society, not God. As if God made a mistake when he created humans to love the same sex. False, God does not make mistakes. The intuition toward homosexuality was written into the homosexuals very heart, very conscience, very fiber, and very DNA. And this must be acceptable to God, if

God is his maker.

The foundational truth here is that mankind is created in the image of God, and therefore fueled by the very energy of God, which is always good. Even the word God has the same etymology with the word good, for the definition of God is that which is good. This goodness and moral decency is there within every man by nature, for all are made of the essence of God. We are his children. Therefore, mankind can rule himself (if the court system were dethroned as the highest authority on morality), for he knows what is right and wrong.

The instant we are told that homosexuality is wrong by society who is listening to the residual principles of an ancient carnal rule (even though it was erased by Christ), we begin to seek justice against this homosexual behavior and the person committing this crime. The foundational belief is wrong. There is no need to change or condemn or judge the homosexual. God made him perfectly, giving him light in his heart. Where the law makes one believe in evil, the truth makes one believe in good.

Let's put Jesus' theory to the test, that mankind knows what is lawful and moral and ethical through the consciousness that was given to the human by God himself. With this philosophy it is declared that a homosexual is perfectly made to be homosexual. In keeping with that same doctrine, one might want to argue then that a murderer was created perfectly to be a murderer. No, that is simply not true.

What is revealed in this philosophy is that mankind is inherently good and perfect. If he or she has done something that our *heart* and *conscience* tells us is morally incorrect, like murder, the conscience reigns and so must be right. Murder is wrong. He or she did not commit murder because he or she is naturally wicked and evil. He or she has committed an immoral act of murder because his or her naturally pure and perfect conscience was contorted, manipulated, or damaged by existential circumstances, beliefs, principles, and fears. It is yet to be seen if in a perfect world which is completely obedient to heart and conscience if homosexuality would remain. It is not yet to be seen if in a perfect world which is completely obedient to heart and conscience if murder would remain.

Here is the difference in these two acts of homosexuality and murder. Let's evaluate what our consciousness says about homosexuality remaining in a perfect world. Pretend that Jesus had simply blotted out the pre-programmed opinion in your mind about homosexuality. Jesus has whited out what was written by the scripture, which was embraced by society, and grew into a monstrous discriminatory practice. Erase that notion and believe that God has not decreed a judgment on homosexuality either way. Ask yourself, are homosexuals harming anyone by committing homosexual acts in their own homes? Are they creating hate or generating love? Is love of any kind a demonstration of darkness, or a demonstration of light?

The truth that is revealed in my conscience today is that homosexuality is love. Love wins and is eternal, because love is the essence of God. On the other hand, murder does not remain in a perfect heavenly society, because death harms. The law of the heart dictates that an act of murder is harmful then. Death, hate, fear, and harm do not follow us into the Promised Land because they are against God/goodness. Death is done away with but love, love of any kind, remains in heaven, according to the true Biblical principles. And so we have been able to make a clear, true, pure decision about the law of homosexuality and the law of murder through trust in our very own hearts and conscience. Homosexuality equals love and so can remain in the heavenly community. Murder harms and equals darkness and can not remain in the perfect community. Does discrimination of any kind remain in a heavenly society? No, discrimination harms and can not remain in a harmonious civilization. That means all carnal laws that create discrimination have to go. Love is the only law here.

One might also argue that someone's conscience might say something different than another person's conscience. Not so. The beautiful thing about this theory is that the same truth that is programmed in my conscience before my birth was programmed in your conscience before your birth by the one and only Creator, therefore our opinions can not vary on what is acceptable and what is not. That same light and truth that is written in me by nature is written in you, because you and I are made of the same living energy (which is the essence of God.) The universe is only made of on substance, living energy, and so every atom declares the same story and the same truth.

To find this original and pure truth that was programmed within us, humanity has to erase all of our preconceived principles that we were indoctrinated throughout many centuries to believe. One must go within oneself, for that is where the kingdom of heaven is found. We must examine our souls, our hearts, and look for that light and that love that we are given by our Creator. Then, the treasure will be found.

Chapter 6 – Love Reigns

In truth, human beings are evolving to a greater understanding (as the Bible states, knowledge shall be increased Daniel 12). In order to arrive to a higher wisdom and greater consciousness and to know decisively and purely without bias what our hearts say, we would need to get rid of irrational notions as decreed by legal and civil dogmas and start with love and goodness as our foundation. Can you see how starting with a foundational system of Old Testament law assumes that one is inherently and naturally evil, and so *must* be governed by outside forces? This is the flaw with the legislative system of the Old Testament.

We must get rid of prejudice and accept all situations, races, colors, creeds, and orientations. We must focus our hearts upon love, for that is what God is and he embodies the highest wisdom. Then, the truth becomes apparent.

Our entire foundational civil structure would begin to be reshaped. A society could emerge where gay marriage wouldn't have to be legalized, it would simply just be marriage without a separate categorization. If churches only knew the truth of their own scripture, they would marry gays because marriage of any kind supports the growth of love. If sports teams and schools and courts and families knew the absolute truth, we would all be set free from the discrimination, the hate, and the racism that plagues and demeans and destroys so many gay lives.

Humanity's unique differences and unique preferences are demonstrated in our reality to teach us to love all without condition (without law, thank you Jesus), not to condemn and hate others for expressing their unique and beautiful qualities. Those who seem 'different' or 'lesser' according to God-Knows-Who's-Standards are placed here on this earth to reveal the very judging and condemning nature of the rest of us. What brave souls are the gay community. Do they arouse feelings of prejudice within you? If so, you are the one who is defiled, because to those that are pure, all things are pure.

In the end, it is prophesied there will be peace on earth. This is only achieved if we accept all peoples unconditionally, isn't it so? Then, when there is no basis for people to feel inferior, degenerate, or hated because of their choices, they are free to live in peace. When there is no basis for other people to feel superior, divine, special, or righteous because they maintain a perfectly holy lifestyle and ostracize the unclean according to an ancient written and carnal law, all can live equally. There is no need any longer to force people into conformity, for God himself has chosen to allow for wonderful diversity, lest the world be a dull and uniform hell.

In summation, once our belief systems change, maliciousness, anger, hostility, pain, suffering, inferiority, and oppression disappear. The Bible says it is principles we fight against, not flesh and blood. Believing the principles of the truth will set us all free. Allowing diversity gains us wisdom and teaches us unconditional love, and so we grow closer to godliness.

In Christianity we no longer condemn to death in our religious practices, so we have taken a step forward. Unfortunately, our legal system still upholds this ultimate punishment. On the same note, we as a people still very much condemn, judge, condescend, demean, and ostracize those that we deem as sinners, which perpetuates the same negative damaging consequence on one's psyche as death. Yes, hating is equated with death as its influence is just as harmful.

1 John 3:15 says, "Whosoever hateth his brother is a murderer."

According to Jesus, we should instead listen to our hearts and conscience and set people free and give them love. Laws like those found all over the Old Testament call for death, making us believe there must be something wrong with the perpetrator of the crime as so we must get rid of them. This is indoctrination. Though we thought that following the laws as given by Moses would earn us eternal life in the Promised Land, they instead have killed the human spirit, human nature, and the human conscience. Romans 7:8 says, "That (the commandments) which was ordained unto life, I found to be unto death."

We have obeyed civil written law as opposed to obeying what God has written in man's heart. One must not harm or steal from another because all humans are worthy of respect and love. Every man's heart knows this, for it is written in him by nature, says the Bible.

Hence, this is the unwritten law we are truly supposed to abide by: Love thy neighbor as thyself *or* Do unto others as you would have done unto you. If you truly loved all as yourself, would there ever be any crime committed against anyone? Would you reject homosexuals if you loved them as yourself?

Instead of abiding by a written law, we are to abide by the voice within. For the kingdom of heaven is within, taught Jesus. Every man knows the inherent beauty, light, and love that resides within his fellow man for every man is created in the image of God. Every man has light and love within, no matter how deeply hidden and contorted that light is by belief in corrupted civil systems and skewed principles of society.

The truth remains. Love is what the heart dictates. Love without conditions, regulations or rules. God doesn't respect a person by his sexual orientation, his deeds, or his behaviors. He judges a mans heart, says scripture. Listen to your heart and do what it says. Love all. This eradicates crime (sin) on one side of the coin and criminals (sinners) on the other side. **You are not going to commit a crime against someone you truly love as yourself. There is also nothing influencing one to commit a crime once the deception of the mind has been eliminated and principle beliefs have been rectified by truth.**

The truth of Christ is that we are all one under

the one God. Though we have the illusion of separateness from God and from each other, the truth is that God is a great spirit or energy, and everything in this universe is created of energy. Period. The same God energy that animates me, animates you, and this is proven now through the unified field theory in science. We are all of the same substance and the same conscience energy.

For one to hate, be prejudice against, or condemn a gay person because God or their 'Christian' religion says it is so, is based on a false belief. That type of racism harms the whole of society as we are all one organism. The damage that is done to one person is done to the whole of society, for the spiritual laws of energy deem this to be true.

Many simply don't know what their religion or their God truly says. They are ignorant. The Bible says, "My people are destroyed for lack of knowledge." The only thing, then, causing pain, suffering, bias, competition, and destruction is lack of knowledge. Even this ignorance is not a crime though, for the Bible predicts that eventually the plan is for all of us to come to the knowledge of the fullness of truth. It takes years of study and deep contemplative meditation or prayer to come to the truth of philosophy in the Bible. But as humanity was enlightened centuries ago in the Age of Enlightenment, so is humanity in the midst of another awakening now. Soon, all will know the deeper truth of how the world works and so will adhere to the teachings of the brightest Light that ever walked the earth – Christ.

God does not judge against any law for that law is fulfilled, rendered powerless, conquered and completed by Christ. God has forgiven all, for he knew we would go through our bumps and our bruises and make mistakes. The truth again is that we are evolving to a higher understanding by trial and error. So this set of governmental systems that the world has adopted has served its time and its purpose. The next step is to revamp everything to the greater wisdom of Christ, Buddha, Gandhi, Krishna – all of these have always known that love reigns supreme.

The truth is that God is love, and he loves all equally, for he is no respecter for persons, says the Bible. If he loves some, but is prejudice against gays, the former statement is not true. He simply does not discriminate.

Get the word out. Now that God's perspective on homosexuality is actually known, society and legislation needs to follow suit. The religious are wrong in their opinions about gays (which is why Jesus called the religious hypocrites, vipers, and serpents). The legislative system which judges people against ancient nonexistent laws is wrong. Understand what Christ came to proclaim. Never would Jesus stand against any human being, no matter, for he and God are no respecter of persons. The law is fulfilled, finished, blotted out, triumphed over, and so there is no law against homosexuality.

In your heart is the truth, and the heart only speaks of love. It is the only language that the heart knows. Hate is not of the heart; it is of the mind or ego. Prejudice is only for the judicial system, which we have just proven is based on un-Christ-like principles. Judgments and prejudices are invalid now that there are no laws to define their framework.

To all family members who are having a hard time accepting the fact that a loved one is gay: Know that society's rejection of the gay community is wrong because society still follows the Old Biblical belief system, as if Jesus never came. Your family member is not deviant or wrong, for there is no law against homosexuality if you believe in Christ and his God. Shame on society for rejecting them and making them feel inferior, for the Western World has no faith in the Christ that they profess.

So gays and all of LGBT- - rejoice! You are loved by God for there is no law against homosexuality. You are completely perfect just the way you are, as your heart has told you all along. I hope this book can help you to justify your love and your unique and beautiful nature against any social and/or religious oppression. Your plight is helping the world to release their laws and preconceived judgments, so that we can all come to a greater truth. Love wins someday soon.

Citations

A Handbook of Bible Law - Foreign Relations, Charles A. Weisman. 2nd Edition: Aug., 1992; 3rd Edition: Dec., 1994, giveshare.org; web

Authorized King James Version Bible, Holman Bible Publishers, 1998, Nashville, TN